James Simmons is regarded
as one of the finest poets of his generation.
He has lectured in Nigeria and at the
University of Ulster, Coleraine, and has also been
Writer-in-Residence at Queen's University,
Belfast.

He founded *The Honest Ulsterman* in 1968
and has also produced four albums of his own songs.
In 1986, *Poems 1956-1986* (Gallery/Bloodaxe) appeared.
His most recent volume of poems is
Mainstream (Salmon).

SOTTO VOCE PRESS

ELEGIES

JAMES SIMMONS

ELEGIES

SOTTO VOCE PRESS
Maynooth
1995

Elegies is first published in 1995
by Sotto Voce Press, Maynooth,
County Kildare, Republic of Ireland.

© James Simmons 1995

A CIP record for this book
is available from the British Library

ISBN 1 873986 05 X

*Sotto Voce Press gratefully acknowledges
the support of the Arts Council of Northern Ireland
in the publication of this book*

Set in Bembo 10 pt
Printed on 135 grammes white cartridge

Design and Origination by Eamon Sinnott & Partners
Cover Photography by Gillian Buckley
Calligraphy by Kevin Honan
Layout by Bill Tinley
Printed by The Leinster Leader

CONTENTS

PREFACE

My first book was published when I was 34, later than most of my contemporaries. That's O.K. It means there is no real juvenilia in print. It also means that my 'selected', unlike that of, say, Mahon and Longley, is a very small part of the whole opus. How different from the case of Seamus Heaney and Paul Muldoon, all of whose volumes are kept in print. Is this the policy of the publisher or the result of popular demand? I can't help regretting that some of my favourite poems, like 'No Land is Waste', are long out of print, and look forward to the day when I find a publisher who will reprint all the old books.

It is fortunate that small presses appear with humility and enthusiasm to save old heroes and foster younger talents. Therefore I am grateful to Sotto Voce for this chance to retrieve lost poems. In this volume some interesting poems will find new circulation, they may even shine brighter in this special context.

Reading Claudel's 'Great Odes' I became aware that I had written many elegies and poems on death that would make a coherent pamphlet ... and they were various in style and technique and content, some informed by sadness or celebration, some satirical or argumentative, some familial, some public. To these I have added one recent long 'Elegy for a Deadborn Child' and 'Derek Kelso'.

The reader will notice the strong influence Auden's 'Elegy for W. B. Yeats' has had on my work, the different ways it allowed him (and then me) to approach a dead person ... and those four beat couplets:

> *Time that with this strange excuse*
> *pardoned Kipling and his views,*
> *and will pardon Paul Claudel,*
> *pardons him for writing well.*

Oddly he left those lines out of his final version! Auden invented a beautiful format that I was able to use for at least three of these elegies. I only noticed recently that Auden was saluting Yeats's 'Under Ben Bulben'. Unlike Auden, Yeats rhymes the whole way through, but he has the same shift from the general and visionary to the homely and particular. Harold Bloom is right that poems are as much about other poems as they are about the apparent subject.

I have not included any poems that appeared in the Gallery/Bloodaxe selection from *Poems 1956-1986* which is still in print. This can be seen as a supplement. 'Elegy for a Deadborn Child' recently appeared in my new collection with Salmon, *Mainstream*.

Going back through all my published works reminded me of the different pressures and experiences that produce changes in style. We live with a head of steam that drives us into the future; but we are not so different from what we were. In the fifties a poem wasn't a poem unless it had its intricate internal rhymes and double meanings and mythological references, and that could produce the sort of manic frivolity that makes W. R. Rodgers, and even Dylan Thomas, now barely readable; but it was also challenging and exciting and good fun. Even then I was also pushing for a sort of cogent plainness. We are in and out and up and down. And being out of fashion for a few years has perhaps been salutary. I never lost my roots in Shakespeare and the ballads.

I've almost never found a book of mine in a second-hand bookshop, and that gives me heart ... that people who buy my books stick with them ... Thank you.

James Simmons

DANGEROUS BATHING

1

DANGEROUS BATHING he must have read
written in black on the white board,
and saw a minor challenge, a rule made
by authority which he ignored.

It meant that python currents pull
strong swimmers down. In his warm ear
waves folded and broke, and sounded cool.
That bit of beach claims someone every year.

Wanting to play with water, he died learning
the sea's a rough companion for a game.
The experience hasn't made him more discerning.
He has no longer got himself to blame.

Without debate he left where I linger
on the empty shore, swam out too far and died.
The murderer, into which I dip my finger,
feels nothing, is not bored or satisfied.

That sign was placed on the sandhills above
by some committee conscious of the dangers ...
a simple memorable act of love
to save their children and their friends, and strangers.

2

Together on scutch grass his parents stand
feeling that murder has been done.
Waves seem evil that break on the cold sand,
since water killed the boy that was their son.

'The foolish, foolish boy. He should have known!'
his father shouts, and stops as they both see
between God's mercy and their own
a terrible discrepancy.

'God didn't punish him,' his wife
says desperately. 'That's not what's meant …
But can God think so little of a life?
Does he let children die by accident?'

3

A sympathetic parson offers reasons
(while big waves canter, a mile below us
across the bay) why at all seasons
good seed drops into those unyielding furrows.

'The world's father gave His only child
to be cut down, then rise up from the tomb.
He had the power to make all fierceness mild
but suffered from the things we suffer from.'

Padre, He played at life! Each wounded hand,
that must have hurt, was just to make precise
points in the contract that His Father planned.
Later He entertained his Friends in Paradise …

and now He referees while we still play
to the bitter end. I think He must be deaf.
'The Lord has given, the Lord has taken away,'
Oh my young men, come, let us kick the ref!

4

So, haunted by their recent expectations,
some men, when they are hurt and frightened, race
from reality, shouting imprecations,
shaking their fists, as though somewhere in space

there was a proper object for their rage.
A wise man knows his father, knows the sea,
learns to endure our dangerous heritage
and use our weapons, love and poetry.

IMPOTENCE

In Memoriam David Mackeral

1

There were nights he would bend to me
and whisper,
'The wee bird sings no more,'
not vulgar,
objectively,
speaking in metaphor.

Solid as the old steam
engines he once
drove, and stout
and stately, he ordered
Guinness and whisky
that I poured out

and carried to him,
to his shrine
in the dark bar
where he waited
benign, smiling,
an Ulster Buddha.

He was well turned out
always. His plain clothes
were impeccable;
but words failed him,
he sat like the frog in the story
at the bottom of a well.

I add these verses
for my mother
who urged me to say
how David,
an old-age pensioner,
paid his way

in the prosperous company
of George the grocer
and my humorous father,
how they teased him,
and how David
was a better man than either.

2

If, years later,
the grown waiter's luck
is such
that beautiful women
like ripe fruit
at the first touch

come away in his hand,
alas, potency
is no longer there,
and the lack in his loins
is reproach almost
too poignant to bear.

He knows,
artful and tender,
that love is a game.
He believes when girls say,
'It doesn't matter, darling.'

But all the same.

3

It's style we remember
people for,
and the craic:
Cleopatra and Antony
and David Mackeral
with the wall at his back.

A great character!
Barflies felt privileged
to stop at his table
and hear his few words,
profoundly slow
and memorable.

And yet,
when Dionysus touched him,
he tried to sing ...
erect, wordless,
tuneless,
self-conducting,

and the drunk youngsters
intuited Black
Velvet Band
or whatever,
applauding,
reaching for his hand.

David seemed to be waiting
for the point
of a difficult joke,
innocent, expressionless,
and then
his smile broke!

Dear old friend,
with all your limitations,
to sing!
Your wee bird could
no more,
and mine is faltering,
was always faltering.

ELEGY

*(Addressed to the Stinson family
on the death of Mrs. Stinson)*

1

I can't advise you
when to dry your eyes.
I can't give shape to the confusion
of your grief, replace the illusion
you don't, enough, believe in.
I only see that death is no stranger;
though stronger than any, not dangerous.
Look him every day in the eyes,
he will come close and not surprise you.
Without violation she is dead,
a house no longer inhabited.

2

As the killer cannot enough
want to control his hands,
each body can only tell
one, its own, story.
There even may be rapport
between a man and the rock
from which he loses his grip
now in the sunlight, although
he cries out, 'No! No!',
as the sun steps back.

3

It is strange how today
a conception can, like a candle,
be lit, and I believe
what I heard often and laughed at, see,
in the tidy huts of a settlement,
heaven, and know Christ well enough
to trust his promise of accommodation.

Are these lit candles of trust
like chestnut blossoms in the heart's field,
or can they blow out in a wind,
or, long prior to the decay of churches
that once were calm and shining,
disappear like other human trifles?
Or will they come back year after year?

4

Her spirit is (this body's hollow)
nowhere or somewhere we won't follow,
wash and lay out with respect
what is now a derelict.
Mourn the loss that has occurred
as her features grow more blurred.
In black or ordinary dress
be happy in her happiness.
We miss her, not in words but there
in the kitchen, on the stair.
In the spring and in the fall
we know the gap is physical.

But in her children will be seen
what she is and what has been,
in a husband and a friend
see that life will have no end,
in grandchildren of the dead
see what they have partly made.
The last children that arise
have Adam's features, Eve's eyes.

5

Let us rejoice then in the death
of a woman no better than she was,
how good only God knows.
Rejoicing and sorrow are not what we say
but our lives now, today.
The effect she has on us,
and we cannot help it,
is the only statue we can erect.
Gone where we cannot see her
or imagine, believe that there
she is better able to read
tide marks and seaweed
on the long shore of God
where we advance and recede.

ATROCITIES

In a field in Germany forced labour
an old Pole cannot do
he keeps just sitting down
the overseer gives orders
two Jews are to dig a hole
they do and put the old man
in and will not bury him

more orders the two Jews
are to get in the hole and they will be buried
by the old man so one of them runs
and a guard stops him and breaks his two
knees with his gun

          before he is tumbled
in again his countryman
must climb out and clear the hole
which is not enormous

          dumb with fear
one man buries the Pole
who is tired and the wounded Jew together
quiet grunts come through the loose
clay for the surviving Jew
is weak and slow

          soldiers stamp
hard the freshly dug ground
it seems mercifully and now
it is time for everyone to go

when I tell this story it always sounds
like a problem in philosophy
inviting a host of permutations
on shame and fear and pain a warning

to never let it happen again
the religious to guess which of these
his creatures god hates most

here in my head is a field near
where I live and I am humiliated
I am a man digging and a man
past suffering pain glad to be dead

THE SUN

for Edward Thomas and Edwin Muir

When we walked, my dear,
from the park last year,
you said, 'There's nothing
like the sun.
Its brightness falling
on trees and walls,
the paths, the grass
and everyone.
It lights the rain-wet
roofs of town,
and finds gold leaves
among the brown.
The sunlight never
shone so sweet,'
you said, last year
in Railway Street.

But I have not,
my love, forgotten,
'There's nothing like
the sun,' you'd say
of September suns
and the suns of March,
October, April,
June and May.
And if you were here
with me today,
'There's nothing like
this sun,' you'd say.
It shines and shines
across the plain:
it will not shine
on you again.

ELEGY FOR J. F. KENNEDY

1

He rose to lead his people, handsome, young,
a face with a new expression, a New England tongue
speaking righteous words – often his own –
too short on pungency and overtone
to be remembered. The presidential car
carried no Caesar, Trotsky, Cromwell, Bolivar;
but the crowds smiled and cheered. They were content
with this one, decent and intelligent.

He talked for, worked for, bought his chance
to mould a nation with laws and influence.

I sometimes think I was born disabused –
The Bay of Pigs was just a giggle. I'm used
to smiling when politicians sweat and swear;
but did a comedian – any comedian – dare
suggest (even in private, the worse for beer!)
there might be that extension to the New Frontier?

Still the do-gooders hailed him, coast to coast,
and cool cynics thought him better than most.
Why was so tough a nation suddenly keen
to accept the evidence of things not seen?
Was this what won the West, sustained the old
frontier? Or just what sent too many after gold?

2

When someone told me Kennedy'd been shot
cold horror took me. Perhaps not
for hopes destroyed; but what had seemed a farce -
remember, 'A politician is an arse ...'
and all that stuff? Old labels didn't fit;
a word gains meaning if one dies for it.
Or so I thought then, and would like to think;
but Hitler died for principles that stink;
and Kennedy's assassin died too ...
we seek his sickness, not his point of view.

3

He came to Dallas, following his mission.
Bang! A bullet cured healthy ambition.
He was planning his next gesture: to throw a kiss,
to smile, to smooth his hair, maybe. Then this.
Rushed in the hands of minions, a president can't die
with the dignity of Orwell's elephant.
The fragile man-machine was quickly broken
too badly for last words to be spoken.
No inspiration can by-pass the fact
that speech requires a respiratory tract.

4

Under Democracy we shouldn't want
a great leader so much as an honest servant
to manage the estate, keep out of war,
balance the budget. That's what they are for.
Gods and, perhaps, heroes are out-of-date.
Compelled by crisis we co-operate,
but hold in our own heads our own fate.

Hitler, Napoleon, Alexander ... they were great,
and I am glad John Kennedy was not,
and sorry the sick man was a good shot.

5

Millions of heads and hands move to create
America; but sorrow is appropriate
for this spilt life. It is proper to bow your head
for a strange hearse as you do for your own dead,
and show the heart's sadness in the face
for all tripped runners in the human race.

DEATH OF A KING

A night with drama students. The party lasted till four
and I woke next morning among bodies on a floor.
One of them turned a wireless on by the bed.
'The B.B.C. offers its sympathy,' it said,
'to Her Majesty and the rest of the royal family.'
And was turned off quietly.

That was the best society I ever knew:
poor students doing what they'd always wanted to do.
The old world died. I stood on the crowded bed
and spoke those stirring words: 'The King is dead.
Long live the Queen.' I seemed to see him standing
among shadows, holding his own hands,
his back almost straight, his head bowed,
as he used to be on occasions above a crowd.
Humble, dignified, simple, not large,
sustained by his kindly people, not really in charge.
He still looked vulnerable, a tame king
not curious to see what death would bring ...
Than wars and politicians no worse thing.

I had laughed at the man, but without malice,
and was touched to think of him leaving his palace
for a journey on which he was not obliged to impress,
alone, unscheduled, lacking fancy dress.
The King was one of those who lived to please us
like Santa Claus and Dr Johnson and Jesus.
He will join them for nectar, sit politely intent
as Hardy scores off God in argument.

My heart was warm. I thought, In the same way
as Hamlet and King Lear, King George is gay.
And stepping over bodies lying prone,
I placed a record on the gramophone;
but the bleary revellers stirred erect,
smelling of cider, and said I might show some respect.
To faces gone solemn I couldn't try
to explain, and put the good record by.

On the bus, at someone's paper furtively peeping,
I was glad to read that he died as he lived – sleeping.

FRANKIE AND JOHNNY GOT MARRIED

They hadn't been married a fortnight
when he said, 'Go on back to your folks.
I can't stand you laughing
when you don't understand my jokes.'

Chorus: Someone here is doing someone wrong.

Frankie and Johnny went drinking.
He talked all night with the boys.
'Johnny, I want to go home,' she said,
'I can't stand all this noise.'

Chorus: Someone here is doing someone wrong.

Frankie had a little baby.
She dressed it all in pink.
Breast-feeding, changing nappies,
there's not much time to drink.

Chorus: Someone here is doing someone wrong.

Frankie said, 'Do you still love me?'
They were lying awake in bed.
'You didn't have to ask that question once,
so something must be dead.'

Chorus: Someone here is doing someone wrong.

Johnny had other women.
Frankie didn't even suspect.
He used to ask her, 'If I laid that girl
do you think our marriage would be wrecked?'

Chorus: Someone here is doing someone wrong.

Frankie's figure was slipping
and every bulge was a bar
on the prison gates, for Johnny thought,
I can't let you go as you are.

Chorus: Someone here is doing someone wrong.

Johnny borrowed a fast car
when the beer was making him burn.
He knew he had no place to go,
and he knew he wouldn't return.

Chorus: Someone here is doing someone wrong.

His foot pressed flat on the floorboard
as the road began to bend;
he shouted, 'I loved you, Frankie,'
just before the end.

Chorus: Someone here is doing someone wrong.

Frankie bent over a new grave
and said, 'I forgive you, my dear.'
A voice said, 'I forgive you too,
so we both stand in the clear.'

Chorus: Someone here is doing someone wrong.

This story has no moral.
Most stories are the same:
there are crimes committed every day
and we don't know who to blame.

BETRAYAL

The dying poet shamed his youth
crying out against the gaudy show,
'Life's plumage fades, life's blossoms go,
not even granite tells the truth.
Love lies like the shiftless snow.'

The need for heaven grows from dearth
of young man's nerve and women's breasts
that still exist when unpossessed,
inhabiting the indifferent earth
with new laughter at old jests.

Though he disowned his warm blunt youth
some men, like Flaubert, Yeats and Joyce,
know they did not grow old by choice.
He called the straws he clung to, truth,
in the distorted quisling's voice.

To use his youth this man had cursed
advice, insurance, any speech
that brought no joy within his reach.
Such spendthrifts are not reimbursed.
No school will hire such men to teach.

But youth cries out as school destroys
what only such as these can give –
worn out, but wise and sensitive.
Old men's true joy is training boys
not to behave but how to live.

DEATH OF A POET
IN BATTLE-DRESS

for George Craig

'I shall forget in 1920
You ever hurt a bit!'
Rupert Brooke

His body was broken. Blood, still pushing round,
fulfilled no function, spilled out on the ground.
He prayed, 'Oh Jesus, please let me fulfil
my early promise, if it be Thy will.'
And I, embarrassed, said, 'What can he do?
Christ may be understood not spoken to.'

He said, 'To me war's crazy, it was the others
brought me here.'
                    I said, 'All men are brothers.'

His right hand held his tunic where he bled,
his left-hand fingers plucked up grass. He said,
'I couldn't lead, I couldn't leave them: trying,
I suffered with them, from them. Now I'm dying,
my good mind never used, and all you see
is a soldier in a uniform, not me.
Help me unbutton this ...' and then he tried
to strip himself. Half-dressed for war he died.

THE IRISH ATHEIST ENDURES
HIS OWN DEATH

'It wasn't his fault,
I always skid in snow.
It isn't a judgment either,
I never could drive.
The doctor says not to move me.
I don't know!
He may be a Protestant.
Yes, I can stay alive
till you run for a priest,
but don't, it's a cigarette
I need. What a woman!
It really never occurred
to her that, dying,
I'd curse the clergy yet ...
ah, but she went for the fags
without a word.'

NOTES FOR A PORTRAIT OF CONRAD

Subjects? The Merchant Navy (Melville's is Whales),
yarns of the seaboard, far-fetched Eastern tales.
A bearded exile, eager to disarm,
in straight jacket navy uniform,
his Polish furies, acting the amateur,
hoping the novelist passenger might, 'endure
my efforts scrawled on ships' bunks off the Cape
or Gib.' Conrad again made his escape,
for the protection of the discipline
of the Merchant Service was wearing thin,
the sea threatening, encroaching more.
That seamless garment stretched from shore to shore
may be for gods but not for men to wear,
too huge and cold. Our element is air
which strangely has the qualities of sea
but softer, spirit in matter, weightlessly
powerful, working on calm water as, say,
thought can convulse a body. Well,
he sat down to write for he had tales to tell,
peace after war, port after stormy seas;
but monsters came to haunt his stories,
fat anarchists, fanatic revolutionaries,
corruption and ambition, boredom, folly,
the yellow streak, the sudden melancholy,
the void. So Conrad, medalled with respect,
much read, warm-housed, securely unshipwrecked,
his beard a landmark on deluxe editions,
had bad dreams. 'The human condition
knits into a fabric decay, despair,
our illusions, the elements, fire, air,
earth and, of course, water.
We are knitted into a fabric, and nothing matters.'

What drove him first across the Polish border –
the double urge for liberty and order –
found him and drove him on, until he saw
return to chaos was the eternal law.
In the red heart of darkness saint and clown,
coolie and captain, all the cowards, lie down.
All contours and connections melt to one
mess under the white-faced sun.

FOR THE CENTENARY

Yeats belongs to the nation, nay, to mankind.
The Irish sell more shamrocks with his fame,
scholars of all shades grub the world to find
facts that mean money in the Eng. Lit. game.

Fame has betrayed him to examinations.
Like Landor, Donne and Shakespeare, Yeats is hated
by schoolchildren – those dying generations:
the captive audience isn't captivated.

In Sligo students gather and take notes
while specialists lecture, cast a frigid eye
on things he mentioned and the grave that quotes
those posturing lines, and then, by bus, pass by.

Surely some newer study is at hand.
When poverty or vanity distresses,
what Ellmann, Jeffares, Henn, his hour come round,
will slouch towards the University presses?

Let strangers, out of Yeats and his affairs,
make souvenirs for sale, relics to hoard.
We will not save or split the poet's hairs
but read his poems, skipping when we're bored.

Fame is the spoor, and vultures won't be baulked
of prey; and yet that voice of Yeats still gives
new friends old thrills. What people chalked
on walls, when Parker died, applies: *Yeats lives.*

THE DAWNING OF THE DAY

Rest easy William Cobbet,
rest easy, William Blake,
and you, wise, gay Lord Byron
who died for freedom's sake.
Rest easy Edward Thomas.
You all have taught the way.
You lived and died to see and speed
the dawning of the day.

Your stubborn courage, Thomas Hardy,
only seemed too mild.
Your lovely jokes were not in vain,
rest easy, Oscar Wilde.
Rest easy D. H. Lawrence,
for you wore yourself away
to spark the fire of life and speed
the dawning of the day.

Rest easy Patrick Kavanagh
and Myles na gCopaleen,
your restless bitchy passions
befit the Irish scene
no less than those of Joyce
at ease in some rich woman's pay.
By devious ways you served and speed
the dawning of the day.

Rest easy in your bitterness
in Ulster now, MacNeice.
Caged by the easy B.B.C.,
pneumonia was release.
That consciousness of having failed
is useful in its way:
the lies of compromise impede
the dawning of the day.

Rest easy Dylan Thomas,
rest easy Geoffrey Hill
(perhaps I shouldn't mention you –
they say you're living still.
But that's no fault of yours.)
We living poets, still at play,
remember you, and memory speeds
the dawning of the day.

WESTPORT HOUSE, PORTRUSH

They have emptied the heart of Westport,
dismantled the great stairwell
and inserted three narrow holiday homes
into the gutted shell
where my parents often welcomed
us children and many beside,
where my children engendered children,
where my father and grandmother died.

Sweet pea, night stock and roses
once made the backyard sweet,
and each year blue lobelia
on the front wall next the street.
Aunt Molly's rosewood piano
was being played all day long.
There was always music. Michael Stephens
began his career of song.

What has happened? No brash invader,
not one soul worth your hate,
but a local builder, a gombeen
with money to speculate,
bought Westport from my former wife
who'd accepted the house in lieu
of alimony. She needed cash
and was lucky to get it too,

for half the slates were missing,
carpets faded and frayed,
the frames of the windows rotting off.
We couldn't afford a maid.
It is hard to sustain a mansion
on a lecturer's modest pay
unless you can make and mend yourself.
It was sinking gradually.

The rusted hinge of the garage door,
where carriages once had passed,
burst from the rotten wood and fell
and was left to die and was lost.
The windows rattled in shrunken frames
and the garden by that late stage
was hidden in briars, weeds and grass
and rubbish flung over the hedge.

Great herring gulls still strut the roof,
eyes bright and hurling down
what sounds like lyrical abuse
that echoes round the town.
There's style and courage in those cries,
ferocious love and hate,
indifference to vicissitude
I cannot emulate.

ELEGY FOR A DEADBORN CHILD

Up stepped the cabin boy and bravely out spoke he.
He said to the captain, 'What will you give to me,
if I will swim alongside the Spanish enemy
and sink her in the lowlands lowlands low,
sink her in the lowland sea?'
The Golden Vanity

1

A brief addition to the family
shown and withdrawn in the longest moment of my life.

all our concern was how to help my wife
endure and survive bearing a dead baby,
all that intrusion, bruising and abuse.

An Indian doctor told us the law said
she must be satisfied the child was dead
before the mother could be treated, induce
labour and get that clot of blood excreted,
remove what now we waited for with dread.

Most of the day we waited.

2

This morning was a holiday. After we woke
we made love. Then suddenly the waters broke.
There should be absolutely no connection
all the doctors insisted. However you thrust
up the vagina the hardest erection
it never troubles the small life held in trust.

The waters broke. The mildest irritation
of wet sheets, and slowly the implication.
The ignorant husband had to be told no embryo
survives the drying up of the amniotic sea.
She gradually brought it home to me.
I had plans for the morning that I must forego.

3

Different doctors on duty had different views,
the nurses made sour faces. It was easy to lose
track. Experts don't always want to say
what they know. Patients are at their mercy.
A corpse in the womb is suddenly dangerous.
The mother is naturally loathe to make a fuss,

pretty and clean in her cotton shift, her mind
grinding to grasp problems, her nerves strained.

Then they came in to inject her. They wheeled her away,
me following, then banished, then restored. I had no say.

'You're doing great, dear,' said a coarse
assistant. 'Push down, hard, to your arse.
Lovely. Push down again, like a hard shit.'

So gods are born. She was glad to be rid of it.

That mind, that body tests the hospital,
nurses and surgeons. In her, nature is ill.
Even the architect, the administration
bear down on her, their skill and limitation.
Nature is fighting nature, their illness fights
her illness. The woman bleeds under the lights.

Four inches long, on folded cotton wool
whatever it was lay,
fleshy, like a pork fillet on a butcher's tray,
skin that transparent
and he pointedly wasn't looking at you,
exact and remote, a small bronze statue.

Closer, his big head was shapely, one arm
folded across a wren-bone chest,
the tiny hands poised, halted
in some activity. No harm
had come to the long fingers, but he was dead.
The little cabin boy had done his best.

We were learning him, like our other little one.
He was like him in miniature, and Ben is small enough.
A brother then, somebody worth mourning.
Mother and father released at last from the rough
mismanagement of hospitals, learning
a sense of loss and reward, to love their son.

5

As we looked and touched
questions were put to us
by nurse and doctor,
how to dispose of this?

To us, tragic and rarely:
to them, unfortunate but daily.
Us, shocked, inclined to hurt,
but resentment was silly.

We could take the thing home,
make of our garden
a private graveyard
with a single headstone,

or make his bed under the roses
or store his ashes in vases,
or leave him lying
where the admin disposes.

Not home surely!
Our bad dog, Charlie,
would smell out meat
and resurrect him early.

We were hard put to decide,
until formaldehyde
the preserver was suggested.
That left us goggle-eyed.

Let the administrator
dispose of the little creature
in whatever usual way,
dustbin or incinerator.

Only in heart and memory
let him survive. Bury him
silent, invisible,
within us, without ceremony.

I always hated magic.
I lost Jesus for that.
Let happen whatever happens,
let the dead lie
stinking of death and life,
finished, flat.
Let all who knew him
exercise memory.
To be born dead
is to be wondered at,
and I wonder.
No one is going to cry.
The wake
will be very private.

Released at last
from that stark theatre,
the steel bowls and blood,
the bleak unhomeliness,
a warehouse, an empty supermarket,

I wheeled you back
to the private bedroom,
its high windows brimming
with green blue sky
of gorgeous evening
after the long day.

We could lie together,
the bruised, bereaved mother,
and her tired lover, semi-conscious
of a pelmet of wispy clouds

being drawn across
the glowing shell of moon.

We were part of the long hot summer of '89
again, exiled in Belfast's Royal Hospital
from our new home by the sea, everything
bad happening and never happier.

My mother
was half a mile away,
down in the City,

slowly and reluctantly
loosing her tough old
hold on life.

8

I drifted back in history,
living another blazing summer,
relished in Donegal
with a different cast
of loved ones, lost now,

one who went off
to England – no bother –
for an abortion
and returned smiling.
She said, 'The day after
we walked down to the station,
three girls with our wee cases.
It was a holiday.'

Janice, you've heard me calling Ben
Charlie, the dog's name, when
I was tired. And Anna, it's well known,
I call by the names of children
with children of their own,
so separate lives get mixed and blend,
Ben and our dead embryo, Helen and Anna.
I like that mystic feel. I cry 'Hosannah'
for birth, for parenthood. Can you let me say,
'Anna is Rachael is Helen is Penelope?'
And I've called you by the names of previous
wives, shuffling my past and duplicating lives.
I stand by this: my mother did the same.
Don't think these quirks insulting or inane,
I was my father, Stewart, to her or my nephew,
Michael, males who at different time she knew
by the one tie of her love, for eternity,
petering out now in Ward 23
in stray smiles, as her mind holds or slips.
I consult my watch, and kiss her withered lips.
Love is confusing, in the surge and relapse
we all fill gaps in other lives and leave gaps
to be filled. Leave my mistakes uncorrected
In confusion the lost lovers are less neglected.
And if you start calling me Don Paul after
your Scottish lover, promise each other laughter
not hurt, embarrassment or accusation.
Bow to the good times. Honour collaboration.

10

Your eyes closed. When your breath was regular
I walked alone down long bright corridors,
unlocked our battered Peugeot and drove home.
Somewhere along the way I stopped involuntarily,
maybe exhausted, and slumped over the wheel,
embracing an old friend who always starts
in the morning and takes us where we have to go.
The son and sister I am driving to
will wait. I sensed above me, above the city
up in the evening sky, something going home,
like one of the lighter planes you see lose height,
down, out of sight, to the harbour. That was my own
son, a failed impulse from the teeming earth
returned, too little, and too lately known.

His mates they dragged him up, and on the deck he died.
They sewed him in his hammock that was so fair and wide,
then they lowered him overboard and he's drifting with the tide,
drifting in the lowlands, lowlands low,
drifting in the lowland sea.

DEREK KELSO

You never went away
though I haven't turned my eyes
after you this many a day,
to your tufty crown and hen toes,
untidy with ambiguities
and stuttering wit, shy but at ease.

I never saw you dead.
You went to the gym, I went for a walk.
Sparring with Clive Bew, you fell, they said ...
and never got up again. We couldn't talk
therefore. I came as close as I could
to you in your box of polished wood.

You and R. P. L. Wells are poised to dive
into the concrete swimming-pool,
him lithe and handsome, you squatter,
lumpier, but at home in water.
Three waifs sent off to boarding-school,
unhappy, happy ... alive.

Your brother, Reggie, tried to ease away
pain at the funeral: 'Derek is looking down
laughing at all this solemn ceremony.'
'Looking down from where?' I snapped, with the frown
of a new-born disbeliever, turning away;
but you were alive in Reggie's mind that day.

My sister tried to cure your lisp;
'You say, "Dethek" instead of Derek?' she affirmed,
helpfully, and you blushed and I squirmed,
hating the intrusion. In anyone's heart
your peculiar speech wasn't a lapse.
For seven years we were seldom apart.

We'd stumble out of the pictures to the Strand Road,
you doing the funny bits till I got a pain
in my chest laughing, and still I'd goad
you on to recycle Bud and Lou in your brain.
In late afternoon sun while the straw was glistening
in horses' dung, I lolled about, laughing and listening.

You've missed 'life' (were inclined to do without it) ...
university, work and marriage, the awful bits
and the wonders. I can say nothing about it
to a boy who danced with his mother. She lost her wits
in grief and anger, when you died, complicating
things that we took for granted, abusing, humiliating
other grown-ups, herself. Your death was a big event.
Without you I have grown up different.